SEP 1 4 2016

# POLYMER CLAY

## *jewelry*

**22 BRACELETS, PENDANTS, NECKLACES, EARRINGS, PINS, AND BUTTONS**

*Sophie Arzalier*

D1379260

## STACKPOLE BOOKS

Lanham   Boulder   New York   London

For my fellow sufferers Fabienne, Marie-Laure, Nathalie, and Stéphanie, whom I wish success on the civil service exam in 2015.

I warmly thank my editor for having given me the opportunity to write this new work.

I also want to thank the readers of my blog, so constant these last years, who have given me the desire to create so many things.

Thank you to Perles & Co. for the materials that made possible the creation of the projects in this book (find them at http:/www.perlesandco.com).

Find Sophie Arzalier @Cristalline
on her blog:
www.cristalline.blogspot.com
at her online store:
www.creations-cristalline.fr
on Facebook:
www.facebook.com/cristalline

Publishing Editors: Isabelle Jeuge-Maynart and Ghislaine Stora
Editorial direction: Catherine Maillet
Editorial coordination: Corinne de Montalembert, assisted by Viki Vileneuve
Graphic design and pagination: Violette Bénilan
Photography: Ayumi Shino
Technique photography and diagrams: Sophie Arzalier
Cover design: Tessa J. Sweigert
Translation: Kathryn Fulton

Copyright © Dessain et Tolra / Larousse 2014
Originally published in France as *Jolis Bijoux en Pâte polymère*

This edition published by
Stackpole Books
An imprint of Globe Pequot
Trade Division of The Rowman & Littlefield Publishing Group, Inc.
4501 Forbes Boulevard, Suite 200, Lanham, Maryland 20706
www.rowman.com

Distributed by National Book Network

All rights reserved. No part of this book may be reproduced in any form or by any electronic or mechanical means, including information storage and retrieval systems, without written permission from the publisher, except by a reviewer who may quote passages in a review. The contents of this book are for personal use only. Patterns contained herein may be reproduced in limited quantities for such use. Any large-scale commercial reproduction is prohibited without the written consent of the publisher.

Printed in the United States of America

10  9  8  7  6  5  4  3  2  1

First edition

**Library of Congress Cataloging-in-Publication Data**

Arzalier, Sophie.
  [Jolis bijoux en pâte polymère. English]
  Polymer clay jewelry : 22 bracelets, pendants, necklaces, earrings, pins, and buttons /
Sophie Arzalier. — First edition.
      pages cm
  Translation of: Jolis bijoux en pâte polymère.
  ISBN 978-0-8117-1656-7
1. Polymer clay craft. 2. Jewelry making. 3. Costume jewelry. I. Title.
TT297.A792913 2015
  745.594'2—dc23
                      2015036383

# Contents

# General Techniques

Polymer clay is a type of craft modeling clay that hardens after about half an hour in a household oven. It is sold in blocks of different sizes and colors, which can be mixed with each other, offering an infinite range of colors. It is easy to work with: You can mold it with your hands or with little tools, add texture with stamps or textured materials, mix in little elements such as sequins, and even decorate it with paint, ink, or patina. In short, the possibilities for transforming this medium are so great it seems impossible to explore them all. This is doubtless what makes it so interesting: There are always new things to discover!

Depending on personal experience, a project that seems simple to some people may seem more complex to others, which is completely normal. Follow your instincts and start with the projects that seem most accessible to you. There will always be time to add complexity to your creations bit by bit when you are more comfortable with this medium. In this book, I give you some easy projects that will help you get started (*) and some that are more complex (** and ***). Without going too fast, take on some projects from a higher difficulty level than you feel capable of—that's how you'll improve!

## WHICH POLYMER CLAY SHOULD I CHOOSE?

### Brands

The choice of brand is important. Far from wanting to convince you to get all your supplies from this manufacturer rather than that one, here I present you with my personal choices and my way of working, based on the experience I already have with these products. The brands I haven't used are not described here, but know there is a wide variety of them out there.

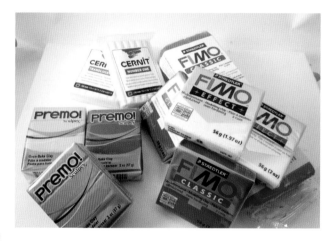

Fimo clay is available in different ranges, according to its consistency and effects: Fimo Soft is very easy to work with, Fimo Classic is firmer; these lines will soon be replaced by Fimo Kid for children and Fimo Pro for adults. The Fimo Effect line includes metallic, glittery, and transparent clays, and Fimo Puppen was created for modeling dolls. I especially like the firmness of Fimo Pro for making projects that use complex canes demanding great precision. The effect clays are very interesting for their variety: translucent, metallic, glittery, or granite. The crumbly look this clay sometimes gets can be fixed by rehydrating it with a spray of water before working with the clay. This clay should be stored in an airtight container to retain all its qualities and suppleness.

Sculpey brand also offers many lines, of which Premo (which includes a range of metallic clays) is very high quality. This brand remains more flexible than Fimo after baking, which can be an advantage or an inconvenience depending on the kind of pieces you want to make; we'll return to this subject.

Cernit clay offers a range of very interesting colors and is very soft and easy to work with. It is therefore perfect for modeling and texture work, but I do not recommend it for making canes, at least not when you're getting started, because the way the canes get squashed when they are cut may be discouraging. Still, the texture is very nice and it takes a very nice imprint of a stamp. These are strong points that cannot be overlooked.

Pardo clay is, in my opinion, the most complete. Its texture and firmness are ideal, and its transparent line is by far the most effective on the market.

Although the basic principle stays the same, each brand offers different physical particularities. I advise you to test several brands and start out working with the ones whose colors and consistency you like best. Thereafter, as you master the different techniques, you can buy different clay depending on the project you want to make: a very soft clay for modeling, a very firm clay for canes, a clay that stays flexible after baking for tiny and fragile reliefs. This is how I make my choice of materials for my creations; I don't have an exclusive brand, since they all have different qualities.

## Special effects

Most of the brands have several color lines available. To the classic opaque colors that are very numerous today are added sparkle-effect colors—these are clays with glitter or mica added to give a metallic effect to their surfaces. There are also translucent clays—not completely transparent—that offer interesting possibilities; they are available in colorless versions and in various colors, and they have a tendency to get darker when baked. Certain brands also have clays with natural looks such as marble or granite, as well as original colors like fluorescent and glow-in-the-dark.

## Pearlescent clay

Pearl clays have a mica base. These particles are like very fine glitter that must all be facing in the same direction to produce their shine—passing the clay repeatedly through a clay machine can achieve this effect. In the photo, on the left is pearl clay that has been worked with a clay machine, and on the right is a block of unconditioned clay; the difference in the look is visible to the naked eye. Moreover, the intensity of the effect is really revealed after the clay is baked and a shiny finish has been added. Go all the way to the end of the process, and you'll be pleasantly surprised (see page 56).

## How do I store the clay?

It is important to know that you shouldn't throw away any "mistakes." All leftover clay, even what has been painted or covered in ink, can be recycled as long as it hasn't been baked. With clay, just as with paint, two colors mixed together will create a new shade. When you just get a brown and don't know what to do with it, you can use this clay to form the inside of round beads and cover the surfaces with pretty motifs.

Polymer clay stores very well over time as long as you follow a few recommendations. You can store your leftover clay in ziplock plastic bags and then put them away in a plastic box with a lid. This way, each color will be separated from the others so they don't stick together, and they will stay good for a long time. Make sure the box is kept somewhere near room temperature or cooler, away from any heat source (sun, radiator, etc.). Be careful not to leave the clay in contact with certain hard plastics or polystyrene, which can cause it to harden.

## Liquid polymer clay

Most of the clay brands offer liquid polymer clay, which has similar properties. Liquid polymer clay comes as a milky gel that becomes translucent or transparent when baked depending on the thickness of the coat. It can be colored with paint or ink, and you can add glitter, seed beads, or other little elements. It also allows you to create glaze effects. You can bake it in a mold, and you can use it as glue to attach an additional piece of clay to an already-baked object. It is not indispensable, but it offers you a new range of techniques to discover.

## Baking

As long as your creation has not been baked, it can be changed and will keep well if sheltered from dust. Therefore, you can wait to fill up a whole pan with projects before baking them. It is only after being baked and allowed to cool that your piece will acquire its final hardness. After this last step, you will obtain rigid little objects that can be pierced, sanded, and varnished, and that can even go through a washing machine. So it is completely possible to make buttons and other embellishments to sew onto clothes. However, avoid covering place settings or decorating cups; polymer clay is not suitable for use with food.

## Conditions

The different brands of clay are all baked at temperatures between 110° and 150°C (230° and 302°F ). This final step in the process can therefore be done very easily and safely in your oven. Later on, if you feel the need because of an increasing rate of production, there will always be time to invest in a little secondhand stove for baking your pieces.

The temperature and baking time depend on the brand, so you should always refer to the instructions on the clay packaging before baking an object. It is imperative to pay attention to this information; otherwise, your piece will be poorly finished. If the temperature is too high, the colors will get darker and the surface may even scorch and emit noxious fumes. On the other hand, if it is too low, your clay will be brittle and crumbly because it was underbaked. Observing the manufacturer's instructions assures a quality product.

Sometimes there can be a difference between the number indicated on the dial of an oven and the actual temperature inside the oven. It is also possible that the temperature may be higher near the internal partitions of a baking tray. In order to avoid unpleasant surprises, it is important to check the temperature with a thermometer.

### Caution

You can find instructions on the Internet vaunting the benefits of baking clay in a microwave or even in water. Know that these methods present risks and clay manufacturers caution against them. Avoid these methods and stick with the classic method of baking in an oven.

## Baking surfaces

Any surfaces that tolerate a temperature of 110° to 150°C (230° to 302°F) can be used for baking your jewelry. For flat pieces, parchment paper, a beer mat, and glass or ceramic trays work well. For curved ones, try glass jars, the bottom of a soda can, a snail mold, or a light bulb. The clay will permanently take the shape you give it when you bake it. You can also bake the clay directly on a jewelry base; this is the case for decorative cabochon pieces for metal bases. You will need to take them off the bases after baking to attach the two components together with epoxy glue.

It is important to limit the number of times the clay is moved while being worked. The best approach is to work directly on the base that will go into the oven. If you have to pull on your project to remove it from your work surface, the newly shaped clay risks stretching out and becoming deformed, especially if you are using a soft clay. Not only does this not look as nice, but it can make your project fragile.

Pierce round beads on a wooden skewer planted in a base of crumpled aluminum foil to avoid an unwanted flat side due to contact with the baking dish. Certain shapes can also be baked in a container filled with baking soda. Be careful that your different pieces don't touch each other, or else they may stick together.

When it comes out of the oven, the clay will still be supple; it will acquire its final rigidity once it is completely cool. Don't forget that some brands, such as Premo, stay a little more flexible than others, which can be an advantage when making fine or thin projects. In this case, the clay will bend under pressure where other types of clay might break. This quality of the clay will also allow you to create little relief details or lacy shapes.

## Characteristics

Polymer clay can be baked multiple times without any worry. The only thing to pay close attention to is the temperature of the oven, which should not surpass the manufacturer's recommendations. The ability to bake the clay several times can be useful for certain projects that require a very firm base before adding the details. Unbaked clay can be attached to a baked piece with a bit of liquid polymer clay applied with the tip of a finger.

## WORKING WITH CLAY

### Work surface

Whatever tools you use for working with your clay or baking it, it is imperative that you keep them only for use with polymer clay. Work on a nonporous surface such as a ceramic tile or a sheet of glass with blunt edges. The clay can be easily detached from these surfaces, and they can be cleaned by simply wiping down with a washcloth.

### Basic tools

For working with clay, you will need at minimum a clay roller and a craft knife. If you plan on working with clay often, you may want to invest in some good specialized blades. You can find them at your local polymer clay retailer, usually in a set of three: a rigid blade, a flexible blade, and a wavy blade. You should be very careful when using this type of tool, and children must be assisted by an adult. Put your knives away carefully after use. Knives can be used to remove bits of clay, to cut blocks into a desired shape, and also to move finished pieces without deforming them. To unstick them from the work surface, simply slide the knife gently between the clay and the work surface and then use the knife to move the piece from the work surface.

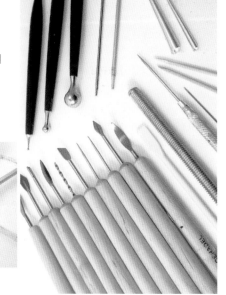

Craft stores also offer assortments of tools for modeling clay and very useful round-ended tools.

You can texture clay with rubber stamps, wood or metal batik stamps, patterned blocks sold for this purpose, or with any other material you find interesting—fibers, synthetic foam, various fabrics, etc.

The reliefs and hollows created in this manner can be colored by simple contact with glittery powders or pigments, such as Pearl Ex, soft pastels, pure pigments, powdered makeup, glitter, or scrapbooking powder.

Paint and inks also work well with polymer clay and expand the possibilities available to you. Try acrylic paint, alcohol ink, metallic ink, stained-glass paint, and other types of paint.

Many different objects can become valuable tools: a wooden skewer or knitting needles for making holes, scraps of fabric and embossed wallpaper for texture, bottle caps for punches, and so on. Learn to look at the objects all around you; they can become interesting and free tools! Also take a look at the baking shelf. Today's decorating trends provide lots of accessories that can be used for polymer clay—textures, little molds, patterned clay rollers, punches in all shapes. Anything can be used to create your own unique projects. Tools can be cleaned with a clean washcloth and soapy water.

## Clay machine

When you're ready to go a little further in your work with polymer clay, the clay machine will quickly become indispensable to you. Beyond allowing you to quickly create gradients, it will save you precious time in conditioning the clay and allow you to make very regular flat sheets of clay in a variety of thicknesses. The machine that I used in making the projects shown in this book is graduated as follows:

1 = 2.7 mm
2 = 2 mm
3 = 1.5 mm
4 = 1.3 mm
5 = 1 mm
6 = 0.8 mm
7 = 0.5 mm

## Conditioning the clay

It is important to condition the clay before you start working with it, even if it is soft when it comes out of the package. You can warm it up between your hands, twist it, then flatten it out with a clay roller or a clay machine. Fold it up and repeat the process several times to obtain a very homogeneous material. The warmer your hands are, the more quickly the clay will become soft.

## TECHNIQUES

## Canes

With polymer clay, you can put different colors next to each other without the colors mixing. This allows you to make what is called a cane—that is, a long snake of clay that contains the same motif on the inside all the way along its length. When you cut slices from this cane, you'll obtain similar pieces that you can then bake as-is or use in a work in progress.

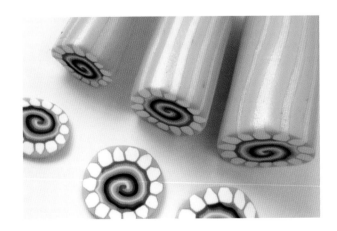

## Working clean

Nothing is more unpleasant than to cut off a piece of immaculate white clay and find that the knife has left behind smears or specks of colored clay. To reduce the amount of finishing work you have to do, clean your tools and work surface often with a clean washcloth.

After baking, small mistakes or unwanted specks can be removed with a cotton swab dipped in nail polish remover.

## Fingerprints

Polymer clay is very sensitive and will preserve faithfully all the textures you apply to its surface—including your fingerprints! Wear fine gloves, or you will need to sand the pieces after baking.

## Attaching embellishments

Holes can be made in clay objects before baking with needles of different sizes, but you can also make holes in pieces after baking using a drill bit turned between your thumb and index finger. Choose your tool for making holes depending on your project; a hole made beforehand will adapt to the surface. Personally, I make holes in round pieces, as well as pieces requiring a rather large hole, before baking, and I prefer to make holes in flat pieces after baking so as not to deform them. Be careful not to drill a hole too close to the edge: Make the hole at least 5 mm from the edge, or you risk the edge of the piece breaking.

Polymer clay does not adhere to all surfaces. If you are working with metal finishings, remove the polymer clay embellishments after they have cooled from baking and attach them to their bases with two-component epoxy glue. Proceed in the same way for rings.

## Sanding

While it is not necessary when you're starting out, a sanded finish gives an undeniable added value to your creations, not to mention that sanding is sometimes indispensable to reveal the beauty of certain techniques. The projects presented in this book can be made without this type of finishing, but I give you a few ideas and tips for when you're ready to try it out.

Sand polymer clay projects with wet sandpaper. This is a special kind of sandpaper that can get wet without losing its grit. Pass it over the baked object with a bit of soapy water. The different kinds of paper are numbered: The higher the number, the finer the grit. You should therefore start with the coarsest grit—400 will work well for smoothing out edges and unwanted reliefs—then go on with a medium, such as 600. If you want to varnish your project, this will be sufficient, but if you want a nice matte finish, you can continue with 1500- and 2000-grit sandpaper. For a professional finish, you'll need to turn to Micro-Mesh® sandpaper.

## Varnish

Although I prefer a matte finish without varnish more and more, varnish must not be neglected. It allows you to protect fragile surfaces such as cracked metal leaf or acrylic ink, and to play with matte-gloss contrasts on a single piece. The products I currently prefer are DTM® lacquer and Darwi brand gloss varnish. The latter is available in gloss and satin and can be applied in one or two coats with a soft brush.

# *Solid-Color Bracelet*
# *Striped Bracelet*

Learn how to make easy bangle bracelets in every color of the rainbow.

**Materials for modeling:**

• Clay machine, clay roller, craft knives, scalpel
• 2 bricks of black or beige clay (for 1 bracelet)
• Scrap of tartalan or other open-weave fabric, or 2 gauze compresses
• Square of plexiglass
• 2 round metal cookie cutters (make the smaller one the inner dimensions you want for your bracelet)

This technique requires a large amount of clay at the beginning, but a lot of it will be left over and can be used to make the brooch on page 14.

## SOLID-COLOR BRACELET

**1** Condition the clay and make three large squares about 2.7 mm thick (setting 1 on the clay machine). Place the first square of clay on the unfolded gauze compress, then add the other two, using the clay roller to force out any air bubbles.

**2** Place the second gauze compress on the top layer of clay. Go over it with the roller to transfer the texture.

**3** Carefully remove the gauze and cut out the center of the bracelet with the smaller cookie cutter, using the plexiglass block to press it into the clay.

**4** Center the second cookie cutter exactly around the hole and cut the outside edge of the bracelet.

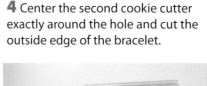

## Tip

If the border is not completely even, smooth it gently before baking.

**5** The bracelet may get stuck inside the cookie cutter. If this happens, don't mangle it trying to get it out, but bake the bracelet inside the cookie cutter. This way, your bracelet will remain perfectly circular.

**1** Condition the clay and make two large beige squares about 2.7 mm thick (setting 1 on the clay machine). Place them on the unfolded gauze sheets.

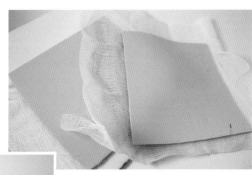

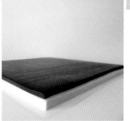

**2** Place a thin sheet of black clay (1.5 mm, setting 4 on the clay machine) on a separate beige sheet 2.7 mm thick (setting 1). Put the whole thing through the clay machine on the thickest setting.

**3** Fold the resulting sheet in half with the beige on the inside and put it through the clay machine again on the thickest setting.

**4** Place this sheet on one of the beige sheets and add the second on top of it. Use the clay roller to work out any air bubbles on each step.

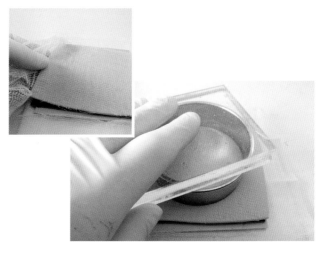

## Tip

If your cookie cutters have joints, align them. This little unevenness in the metal will misalign the black lines for about 2 mm, and it will be easy for you to hide this little defect if these two marks are aligned.

**5** Continue as for the solid-color bracelet, starting from step 3.

# BLACK BRACELET WITH BEIGE STRIPES

**1** Place a fairly thin (1.5 mm, setting 4 on the clay machine) sheet of black clay on a 2.7 mm (setting 1) sheet of beige clay.

**2** Put the whole thing through the clay machine on the thickest setting and cut it into three squares the size of the larger cookie cutter.

**3** Place one of the squares on an unfolded sheet of gauze with the beige side down, then add a second square.

**4** Use the clay roller to squeeze out any air bubbles.

**5** Place the last square on top, still with the black side up, and use the second gauze square to texture the surface.

## Tip

For a nice finish on these striped bracelets, you'll need to sand the outside and inside edges. Use a piece of wet sandpaper and work in soapy water. Sand the edges first with 400-grit sandpaper, then with 600-grit sandpaper until the lines are perfectly clear. For a nice matte finish, you can sand them one more time with 1000-grit paper. The gauze texture can be given a patina with paint after baking.

**6** Continue as for the solid-color bracelet, starting from step 3. To hide the unsightly mark from a joint in the cookie cutter, cut a strip of striped clay from a scrap piece and wrap it around the bracelet. Smooth it out and bake again.

# Striped Brooch

## PETAL CANE

**1** Once you have cut out the center of the striped bracelet, you will have a circle of clay left over. Cut four arcs off the sides of the circle to create a square.

**Materials**

- Striped block: use the center piece left over from a bracelet
- Flat brooch base
- Craft knives
- Flower cookie cutters of different sizes
- Two-component epoxy glue

**2** Form a cylinder of black clay and pinch it along one long edge.

**3** Wrap the striped square around the black cylinder and bend it so that it forms a petal shape.

**4** Pinch the point of the piece firmly all along the long edge.

**5** The cane you just made will serve as the petals of the flower. You can vary the dimensions by stretching out the cane with your hands: The thinner the cane, the smaller the petals will be. When the cane is your desired size, cut five petals 2 to 3 mm thick. Take your time to cut nice, even pieces.

## THE FLOWER

### Tip

You can make pretty floral rings following this same method. Just glue the base of the flower to a ring base instead of a brooch base.

**1** Cut out a circle 2.7 mm thick (setting 1 on the clay machine), as big as the brooch base, and attach the petals on top of it.

**2** In the center, place a flower cut from a thin sheet of beige (or black) clay with a cookie cutter, then a smaller black (or beige) flower on top of that. Bake according to the manufacturer's instructions. After the piece has cooled, glue the flower to the brooch base with a strong adhesive.

# *Tale of Africa Necklace*

Create jewelry with a rugged, natural look by stacking chips textured on front and back.

**Materials
for making the beads:**

• Clay machine, clay roller
• Needle for making holes in the beads
• Woven gauze compresses
• 6 small round cookie cutters: 0.7 cm, 1 cm, 1.1 cm, 1.3 cm, 1.5 cm, and 1.6 cm (¼ in., ⅜ in., ⁷⁄₁₆ in., ½ in., ⁹⁄₁₆ in., and ⅝ in.) in diameter
• 1½ bricks of crimson clay and ½ brick of red clay
• Small amount of gold Pearl Ex (or eyeshadow)

## MAKING THE CHIP BEADS

**1** Condition the crimson clay and make a thin sheet of it (1.5 mm, setting 4). Wrap the sheet in gauze and put the whole thing through the clay machine.

**2** Cut out the chips with a cookie cutter, leaving both pieces of gauze in place. For a long necklace, make 180 beads 0.7 cm (¼ in.) in diameter, 42 beads 1 cm (⅜ in.) in diameter, 42 beads 1.1 cm (⁷⁄₁₆ in.) in diameter, 42 beads 1.3 cm (½ in.) in diameter, 42 beads 1.5 cm (⁹⁄₁₆ in.) in diameter, and 42 beads 1.6 cm (⅝ in.) in diameter in crimson red. Make 10 beads 1.6 cm (⅝ in.) in diameter in bright red.

**3** Remove the top compress and gently remove the clay from around the beads.

**4** To remove the beads and give them their shape, stretch out the remaining gauze compress diagonally in both directions by pulling with your hands. The beads will detach themselves on their own.

## Tip

For a longer necklace, increase the number of small beads: 1 cm (³/₈ in.) of length = about 6 beads.

**5** Pierce holes in the centers of the beads.

### MAKING THE CONTRASTING FLAT BEADS

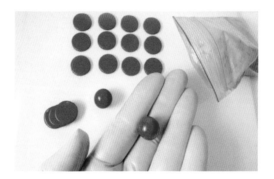

**1** Condition the remaining quarter brick of red clay and make a thick sheet from it (setting 2). Cut out three disks 1.5 cm (⁹/₁₆ in.) in diameter. Roll the clay in your hands to form seven round beads.

**2** Rub a bit of gold powder on your hands and roll the beads again to give them a bit of flash.

**3** Cover both sides of the beads with the gauze compresses and press with a plate or other flat surface to mark the texture into the clay and to lightly crush the beads. Make holes in the centers and bake.

**Materials
needed for assembly:**

- 1 m (1 yd.) of beading wire
- 4 crimp beads
- 2 beading grommets
- 2 seed beads 4 mm in diameter
- Small extension chain, 2 jump rings 0.6 mm in diameter, 1 lobster claw clasp
- Pair of cutting pliers, 2 pairs of flat pliers

**1** Pass the end of the beading wire through the grommet and secure it with a crimp bead.

**2** Add a seed bead and a second crimp bead.

**3** Thread on the clay beads in ascending size order until the central bead, then in descending size order, and so on around the necklace.

**4** Add another crimp bead, a seed bead, a crimp bead, and the grommet.

**5** Bring the beading wire back through the last three elements, and crimp the crimp bead.

## Tip

To open and close a jump ring, use two pairs of pliers.

**6** Cut off any extra beading wire. Attach the chain and the clasp with the jump rings. The gauze compress will have left multiple very fine lines on the edges of your beads. Singe them with a lighter using a rapid gesture.

# Bright Flowers Necklace

Create floral relief beads with just small balls of colored clay.

**Materials
for the necklace:**

- ¹/₄ brick each of violet, pink, green, and gold polymer clay
- Needle for adding texture, small palette knife
- Round cookie cutter 4 cm (1¹/₂ in.) in diameter
- Round cookie cutter 1 cm (³/₈ in.) in diameter
- Gold Pearl Ex or gilding wax
- 12 bronze rings 8 mm in diameter
- Rigid craft knife

## NECKLACE

**1** Condition the violet clay and form it into a thick sheet (2.7 cm thick, setting 1). Cut out three circles 4 cm (1¹/₂ in.) in diameter with the cookie cutter. Cut each shape into two parts with the rigid knife.

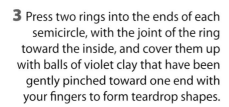

**2** Condition the violet, pink, and green clay, and make thin, regular ropes from them by rolling the clay on the work surface. Cut each rope into little even sections and make them into balls a few millimeters in diameter.

**3** Press two rings into the ends of each semicircle, with the joint of the ring toward the inside, and cover them up with balls of violet clay that have been gently pinched toward one end with your fingers to form teardrop shapes.

## Tip

To obtain very regular ropes in step 2, you can use a clay gun or a garlic press reserved for this use.

**4** Texture these teardrops with a needle so that each adheres firmly to the base.

**Materials
for assembly:**

- 2 lengths of bronze chain 14 cm (5½ in.) long, clasp, large ring 8 mm or 1 cm (³∕₈ in.) in diameter
- 8 bronze jump rings 4 mm in diameter

**5** Next place the pink shapes, then the green ones.

**6** Cut out three gold circles with the 1 cm (³∕₈ in.) cookie cutter and add texture lines to the surfaces with a needle or palette knife. Cut them in half and place them in the center half circle of each bead.

**7** Use the tip of your finger to brush a little bit of gold Pearl Ex on the raised portions of each bead, and bake the six beads on a piece of cardboard.

## ASSEMBLING THE NECKLACE

Simply attach the beads together with the 4 mm jump rings. Then attach the chain and clasp to finish the necklace.

# Tip

If after the pieces have cooled the gold on the reliefs isn't pronounced enough, you can enhance the effect by applying a bit of gilding wax or acrylic paint in the same color with the tip of your finger.

# Bright Flowers Button

✳✳

**Materials
for the button:**

- ¼ brick violet polymer clay
- ¼ brick fuchsia, ⅛ brick green, and a small amount of gold
- Needle for adding texture
- Cookie cutter 4 cm (1½ in.) in diameter
- Gold Pearl Ex or gilding wax
- Clay gun with an attachment for creating narrow ropes (optional)

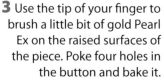

**1** Prepare little teardrops of violet, pink, and green clay as for the necklace (step 2). Cut a 4 cm (1½ in.) circle from a thick sheet (2.7 cm, setting 1) of clay. Place the teardrops around the edge of the circle. Mark each petal with a needle.

**2** Work in this same way with the green and pink clay, working toward the center. Finish with a flattened ball of gold clay, drawing patterns in the center with the needle.

**3** Use the tip of your finger to brush a little bit of gold Pearl Ex on the raised surfaces of the piece. Poke four holes in the button and bake it.

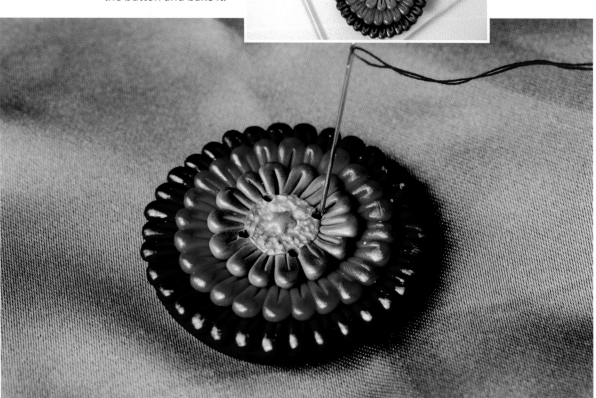

# ❋ Poppies

Discover a simple method for making flowers from very little material. By recreating this pattern with more petals and different colors, you can produce an infinite range of creations.

**Materials
for 4 buttons:**

- 1 brick of red polymer clay
- ⅛ brick of green clay
- Small ball of glittery black clay
- Acrylic paint in burnt umber
- Round cookie cutter 3 cm (1 in.) in diameter
- Needle
- Palette knife

## BUTTONS

**1** Cut out a circle from a sheet of red clay 2 mm thick and cut it into four pieces. Shape the outer borders with the needle. To limit the risk of deforming the petals, work directly on the surface that the petals will be baked on.

**2** Round out the corners of each petal, then texture the surface by creating fine lines with a needle.

**3** Make a little ball of glittery black clay, shape it into a teardrop, and place it at the base of a petal. Use a needle to spread out and texture the clay.

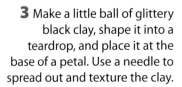

**4** Use the cookie cutter to cut a circle from a medium-thick sheet of red clay. Place the petals on it and stick the base of each firmly to the clay without crushing it. Gently bend up the corners of the petals.

**5** Add a little ball of green clay at the center and press lightly with the palette knife to create a star mark in it.

**6** Use a needle to poke four holes around the center of the flower. Bake the buttons, then add a patina to each center by spreading a thin coat of burnt umber paint over it and wiping it off right away.

## ✹✹ Poppy Earrings

**Materials
for assembling the earrings:**
- Small flower cookie cutter 1.5 cm (⁵⁄₈ in.) across
- 2 fine metal rings 3 cm (1 in.) in diameter
- Flat pliers
- 2 ear wires

**1** Use the cookie cutter to cut two flowers from a thin sheet of green clay. Gently bend up the tip of each petal.

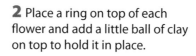

**2** Place a ring on top of each flower and add a little ball of clay on top to hold it in place.

**3** Attach the petals two by two, pressing lightly on the centers.

**4** Add a small ball of green clay in the center and use a palette knife to create a star pattern in the center, as in step 5 for the buttons.

**5** Shape the petals, curving them upward and overlapping them to keep them in place. Bake the pieces, then apply a patina to the centers with acrylic paint, as in step 6 for the buttons.

## Tip

If pressing the petals diminishes the texture, you can touch it up with a needle.

**6** Finish the earrings by simply attaching an ear wire to the metal ring.

# Pink Candy Bracelet

A bracelet in neon candy colors! Play with the opacity and translucency of the clay with a cookie cutter.

**Materials for making the beads for the bracelet:**

- Fuchsia pink, pale pink (fuchsia + white), translucent red, and violet clay
- 6 silver eye pins 4 cm (1½ in.) long
- 12 little white seed beads
- Round cookie cutters 1.9 cm (¾ in.) and 1.5 cm (⅝ in.) in diameter

## MAKING THE BRACELET

**1** For the bases of the beads, cut out six rounds 1.9 cm (¾ in.) in diameter in assorted colors (from a thick sheet, setting 1) and place them on a piece of cardboard.

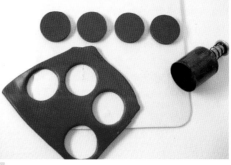

**2** Mark the placement of the eye pin by pressing it into the clay. Cut six rounds 1.5 cm (⅝ in.) in diameter for the tops of the beads.

**3** Place a seed bead on the eye pin, then place a bead top in the center before placing a second seed bead on the end.

**4** Place this assembly on the base of the bead, with the eye pin between the two layers of clay, and press the two parts together. Bake without closing up the pin loop so that the pieces don't become misshapen.

# Assembling the Bracelet

**Materials
for assembling the bracelet:**

- Flat pliers, cutting pliers, needle-nose pliers
- 5 round pink and violet beads 6 mm in diameter
- 15 head pins 2 cm (¾ in.) long
- 5 violet seed beads 4 mm in diameter
- Small mauve and white seed beads
- 5 small pink crystal butterfly beads
- Toggle clasp
- 7 jump rings 6 mm in diameter

**1** After the pieces have cooled, bend the eye pins at a 90-degree angle with the flat pliers and cut the wires 7 mm from the angle.

**2** Use the needle-nose pliers to bend the remaining wire into a horizontal loop.

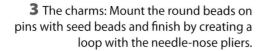

**3** The charms: Mount the round beads on pins with seed beads and finish by creating a loop with the needle-nose pliers.

**4** Proceed in the same way for the little butterflies. On other pins, thread on different seed beads for a length of 1 cm (⅜ in.).

**5** Attach two polymer clay beads together with a jump ring, adding one charm of each type before closing up the ring.

**6** Finish by attaching the two parts of the toggle clasp with jump rings.

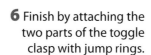

# *Pink Candy Earrings*

**1** Make two polymer clay beads as for the bracelet and attach them to the ear wires.

**2** Open the ring on the bottom of each bead and attach the three charms.

**Materials
for the earrings:**

- 2 polymer clay beads like those used for the bracelet
- 2 ear wires
- 2 round glass beads in pink and violet 6 mm in diameter
- 2 eye pins 2 cm (³/₄ in.) long
- Violet seed beads 4 mm in diameter
- Small mauve and white seed beads
- 2 small pink crystal butterfly beads

# ✱ Confetti

Making a cane might seem really complicated when you're starting out. Here, you'll learn a very simple version of this technique to use when creating tube beads.

**Materials
for making the buttons:**

• White, black, and red clay
• Clay gun and attachment with little holes
• Plexiglass sheet
• Small glass square
• Rigid craft knife, large needle

## BUTTONS

**1** Condition the three colors of clay separately, starting with the white and finishing with the black. Put them one by one through the clay gun with the little holes attachment mounted on it to create lots of little ropes of identical size.

## Tip

If you don't have a clay gun, slowly roll out a long rope in each color. For a more even thickness, roll the ropes under a piece of glass or a tile.

**2** Place the ropes of clay together, mixing up the colors. Form them into a flat log: You've just made what is known as a cane.

**3** Cut this cane into two equal parts and put these parts together to form a cylinder.

**4** Smooth out the outside edge by rolling the cane on the work surface with the plexiglass block, then wrap a thin (setting 4) sheet of black clay around the whole thing.

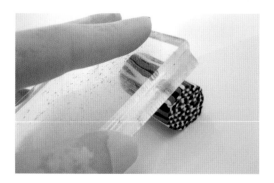

**5** Smooth out the cane again and shape it into a slab by pressing the cane between the work surface and the plexiglass.

**6** Wait at least half a day before cutting your cane into slices of equal thickness, as this will reduce deformations. Shape the cane back into a square as needed if it gets squashed while you are cutting it. To get very smooth buttons (and to fix their thickness if it's uneven), press them with a square of glass sprayed with water. Poke holes in the buttons with the large needle and bake them.

# Paper Lantern Pendant

## TUBE BASE

**Materials for the tube bead:**

- Craft knives, clay machine, clay roller
- Red, black, and white clay
- Scraps of leftover clay
- Knitting needle (without a cap on the end)
- Clay gun and attachment with little holes
- Block of plexiglass
- Flower cookie cutter 2.5 cm (1 in.) across

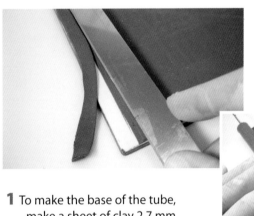

**1** To make the base of the tube, make a sheet of clay 2.7 mm thick from leftover clay and cut one edge on a diagonal.

**2** Place the knitting needle on the beveled edge and roll the clay up around it.

**3** Make sure the needle is exactly in the center, then cut the other end of the sheet on a diagonal before finishing the roll.

**4** Roll this log on the work surface until it is 1 cm (³/₈ in.) in diameter.

**5** Cut the log into fourths, then place one of the pieces back on the knitting needle; this way you can work on the bead without crushing the hole. Condition the three colors of clay separately, as for the buttons, starting with the white and ending with the black. Put them one by one through the clay machine with the little holes attachment to produce lots of little ropes of identical size.

# DECORATIONS AND ENDS OF THE TUBE

**1** Make a polka-dot cane, as for the buttons, but stop before cutting it in two. Choose the style you prefer for your pendant: either cut slices from the cane, put them around the center cylinder, and smear slightly with your fingers; or wrap the ropes around the cylinder candy-cane style.

**2** From a thin sheet of black clay (setting 6), cut two flowers with the cookie cutter.

**3** Place the cylinder end in the center of a flower, and fold the petals down over the decorated part.

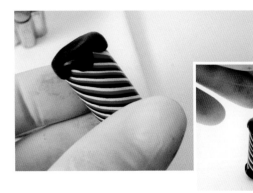

**4** Use the needle to poke a hole in the center. Make three more pendant beads, if desired. Bake the beads.

## ASSEMBLING THE PENDANT

**1** Use the ribbon to attach the pendant to the large jump ring. Use a piece of beading wire folded in half to thread the ribbon through the bead.

**Materials for assembly:**

- Matching ribbon, piece of beading wire
- Closed metal jump ring
- 2 imitation suede cords 45 cm (18 in.) long
- 2 silver cord ends, 2 rings, clasp

**2** Fold each cord in half and attach it to the ring with a loop.

**3** Attach the cord ends to the cords and add the clasp. Singe the ends of the ribbons and secure the knots with a dot of glue.

35

# Stone Buttons and Ring

"Stones" that imitate natural minerals are easy to make with granite-look and translucent clays. This trio of stones can be glued onto a support to make a ring or can have two holes added to become a button.

**Materials needed for modeling:**

- 1 brick of granite-look polymer clay
- White and translucent clays
- Large needle for poking holes
- White embossing powder (optional)
- Round cookie cutter 2 cm (3/4 in.) in diameter
- Plexiglass block
- Dark acrylic paint (black or brown)

## MODELING

Natural-effect clays can be used as-is; however, for a more varied and realistic look, follow these steps to create a marbled effect and surface irregularities.

**1** Condition the granite clay and make it into a cylinder. Twist two thin ropes of white and translucent clay together, fold in half, and twist again.

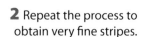

**2** Repeat the process to obtain very fine stripes.

**3** Place these white stripes of different sizes on the top and bottom of the granite cylinder.

**4** Roll the cylinder on the work surface to lengthen it out, fold it in half, and twist it to accentuate the irregularity of the white lines.

**5** Form the piece into a long log and apply a bit of embossing powder to it in a random fashion (optional).

**6** Roll the log under the plexiglass square to press the embossing powder into the clay.

**7** Cut off sections of the size desired for your stones and pinch the ends to round out first one side, then the other.

**8** Roll each piece between your hands and flatten it with your palms to give it the shape of a small stone.

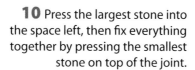

**9** Make three stones of different sizes and cut out part of the medium one with the cookie cutter.

**10** Press the largest stone into the space left, then fix everything together by pressing the smallest stone on top of the joint.

## ASSEMBLING THE BUTTONS

**1** To make varied buttons, follow the steps above to make several stones.

**2** Make holes in the stones before baking with a needle or after baking with a drill bit.

**3** Bake as directed, and once the stones have cooled, apply a patina to the crevices of the stones with a bit of dark acrylic paint, wiping it off immediately with a paper towel.

## ASSEMBLING THE RING

**1** Bake the stones as directed, and once the stones have cooled, apply a bit of dark acrylic paint to the crevices, wiping it off immediately with a paper towel.

**2** Clean any parts with too much color with a cotton swab dipped in rubbing alcohol, as needed. Let dry.

Materials
for assembling the ring:

• Two-component epoxy glue
• Flat-topped ring base
• Black or burnt umber acrylic paint
• Liquid polymer clay
(for the back of the ring only)

**3** Glue the ring base to the bottom with two-component epoxy glue.

**4** Let dry for the time indicated. Put a little bit of liquid polymer clay on your fingertip and spread it on a small sheet of clay that has had a hole cut in the middle and the side sliced through, as shown in the photos. Attach this piece of clay between the ring base and the stone.

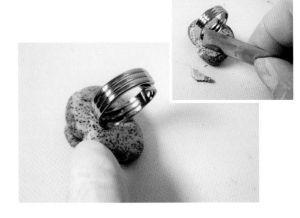

**5** Make sure it adheres well, then cut off any surplus with a craft knife and smooth out the joints. Bake again, following the manufacturer's recommendations.

# *Buttercream Necklace*

Put together little bits of colored clay to create polka-dotted and striped beads. These go together well with a lace texture with a white patina.

**Materials for the necklace:**

- 1 brick of beige polymer clay
- 1 brick of white clay and a little bit of black clay
- Clay roller, craft knife
- Scrap of lace for texture, gauze compress
- Round cookie cutters 3.8 cm (1½ in.), 3 cm (1⅛ in.), 2.3 cm (⅞ in.) and 1 cm (⅜ in.) in diameter
- 2 butterfly cookie cutters 2.5 cm (1 in.) and 1.5 cm (⅝ in.) across
- Small circular punch, wooden skewer, graph paper, needle
- Plastic food wrap, cellophane
- White acrylic paint
- Sheet of plexiglass
- Baby wipe

## STRIPED BEADS FOR THE NECKLACE

*Make three: one 3.8 cm (1½ in.), one 3 cm (1⅛ in.), and one 2.3 cm (⅞ in.).*

**1** Condition ¼ brick of white and make a medium-thick (setting 2) sheet, which will serve as the base. Place it on the gauze. Next prepare ⅛ brick of medium thickness in white, beige, light beige (mix beige and white), and gray (add a bit of black to beige).

**2** Cut strips of different widths from each of the prepared colors and place them randomly on the base sheet. Use the flat of the craft knife to press the strips together.

**3** Smooth out the joints between the colors with the tip of your finger through a sheet of cellophane, following the direction of the lines.

**4** Leaving the cellophane in place, put the whole thing through the clay machine (on setting 1), still in the direction of the lines.

**5** Next, cut out your beads and place them on the baking surface.

# POLKA-DOTTED BEADS

*Make three: one 3.8 cm (1½ in.), one 3 cm (1⅛ in.), and one 2.3 cm (⅞ in.).*

**1** Condition ½ brick of white clay and make a thick sheet (2.7 cm, setting 1) which will serve as the base.

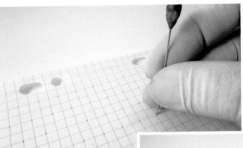

**2** Place a sheet of graph paper on the clay and mark the placement of the polka dots with a needle.

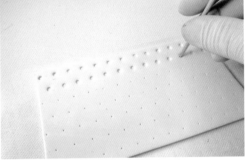

**3** Remove the paper and, with the flat side of a wooden skewer, deepen the marks for the placement of the dots. This step will ensure that they don't become deformed when the clay is smoothed out.

**4** Take a bit of beige clay and make a thin sheet (setting 5), then cover it with a sheet of plastic food wrap.

**5** Use the punch to cut out as many dots as needed, then remove the plastic food wrap.

**6** Remove the dots with the tip of a needle and place them on the marked spots on the white sheet.

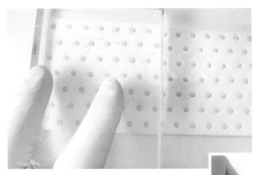

**7** Place a piece of cellophane on the clay and press with a piece of plexiglass, then gently roll it out, in both directions, without deforming the dots. If the white clay gets dirty as you work, you can gently clean the surface with the baby wipe.

**8** Cut out the circles and butterflies with the cookie cutters. Bake.

## Tip

If you don't have a punch of the right size, glue an eyelet to the end of a stick with a bit of super glue.

## LACE BEADS

*Make three: one 4.8 cm (2 in.) and two 2.3 cm (⅞ in.).*

**1** Condition half a brick of beige clay and make a thick sheet from it (2.7 cm, setting 1) and place it on the gauze compress. Cover the piece with lace with the more raised side facing down on the clay. Go over the lace with a clay roller to press the pattern into the clay.

**2** Cut out circles with the cookie cutter and place them on the baking surface.

**3** After the pieces have baked and cooled, paint the lower surfaces with white acrylic paint and wipe off the raised surfaces with a paper towel. Let dry.

43

# ASSEMBLY

For this assembly, you will need to make holes in the flat beads about 4 mm from the edge and also make holes right through the cord, directly below the beads. From this point, the metal pins will thread very easily through the rubber.

**Materials for assembly:**

- 12 ball-style head pins 2 cm ($^3/_4$ in.) long
- 4 flat head pins 2 cm ($^3/_4$ in.) long
- 1 silver bead cap
- 45 cm (17 $^3/_4$ in.) of transparent rubber 4 mm in diameter
- 2 large cord ends, 3 rings, clasp, extender chain
- Tassel made of white fibers
- 1 mm drill bit
- Flat pliers, cutting pliers, needle-nose pliers

**1** Make beads in the following diameters: one lace bead measuring 4.8 cm (2 in.) and two 2.3 cm ($^7/_8$ in.); one striped bead measuring 3.8 cm (1$^1/_2$ in.), one 3 cm (1$^1/_8$ in.), and one 2.3 cm ($^7/_8$ in.); one polka-dotted bead measuring 3.8 cm (1$^1/_2$ in.), one 3 cm (1$^1/_8$ in.), and one 2.3 cm ($^7/_8$ in.). Cut out one medium butterfly and three little ones.

## Tip

To easily drill through the beads and the cord, use a 1 mm drill bit.

**2** Start at the center of the rubber tube and attach the largest flat bead there: Make two holes in the bead, 4 mm from the edge, and make two holes through the tube, keeping the same distance between the holes.

**3** Make a hole through the little striped bead, at one edge, and attach it to the large bead with a ball-style head pin, passing the pin through the cord as well.

**4** Bend the end of the pin at a 90-degree angle on the back to hold your work in place.

**5** Add the 3.8 cm (1$^1/_2$ in.) polka-dotted bead on the right and the large butterfly on the left; continue to assemble the necklace in the order shown in the photo at left.

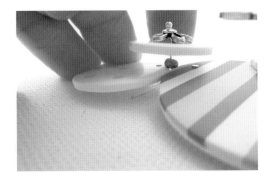

**6** The little butterfly on the right and the little polka-dotted bead with the flower bead cap are raised by a large (4 mm) seed bead underneath. Use flat head pins for the beads underneath these two pieces.

**7** Once all the beads are in place, cut the pins on the back 0.5 mm from the tube and bend the ends back with the needle-nose pliers to eliminate any sharp ends.

**8** Attach the cord ends to the ends of the rubber cord, then attach the clasp and the extension chain decorated with a little polka-dotted butterfly.

**9** Add the tassel under the large butterfly and cut the fibers to the desired length.

## ✱ *Buttercream Earrings*

Drill holes in the centers of the butterflies and 4 mm from the edges of the round beads. Pass the large rings through these two holes and add the large seed beads. Attach the ear wires with the small jump rings.

**Materials for the earrings:**

- 2 round lace polymer clay beads 3 cm (1⅛ in.) in diameter
- 2 mini polka-dotted butterflies
- 2 large open jump rings 8 mm in diameter; 2 small open jump rings 4 mm in diameter
- 2 ear wires
- 2 large gray seed beads 4 mm in diameter

# *Ice Queen Necklace*

With this project, you'll learn how to make a necklace from large hollow beads—an impressive but lightweight effect. The beads in this necklace can also be worn on their own, as pendants.

**Materials
for making the beads:**

- Craft knife, clay roller, or clay machine
- 7 cotton balls 3 cm (1⅛ in.) in diameter
- 1½ bricks white polymer clay
- ¼ brick silver polymer clay
- Silver ink or acrylic paint
- Round cookie cutter (or eyelet) 1 cm (⅜ in.) in diameter
- Flat-back rhinestones of different sizes
- Small crochet hook
- Gem glue
- Coarse salt

## HOLLOW NECKLACE BEADS

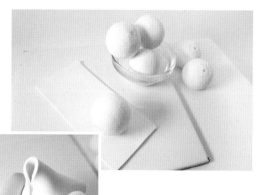

**1** Make a white sheet of medium thickness (setting 3) and cut out six rectangles 5 x 10 cm (2 x 4 in.). Roll each cotton ball up in a clay rectangle, taking care not to trap any air inside.

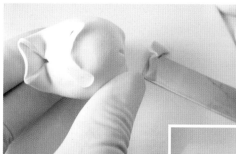

**2** Pinch the excess clay together and cut it off with a good craft knife.

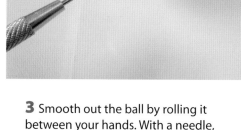

**3** Smooth out the ball by rolling it between your hands. With a needle, make a hole from one side to the other to mark the axis.

**4** If you notice any air bubbles, squeeze them out through one of the two holes. Roll the bead in the coarse salt until the surface is uniformly textured. Add a bit of salt to any areas that need it.

**5** With the small cookie cutter, cut the holes out properly around the positions you marked with the needle.

## Tip

If you don't have a small cookie cutter, use one of the eyelets.

**6** Remove the surplus.

## Be careful!

Follow the manufacturer's baking times and temperatures! If your beads are not fully baked, they may break when you remove the insides, and if the temperature is too high, the white clay may get burnt.

**7** Repeat the process for the seven balls. Apply a bit of silver ink to the raised areas of the last ball. Bake according to the manufacturer's instructions.

**8** After baking, soak the beads in water for at least an hour to dissolve the salt and soak the cotton.

**9** Use the crochet hook to completely remove the cotton from inside each bead.

**10** Rinse the beads under a faucet and let dry. Use the gem glue to attach the flat-back rhinestones to the silver bead. Glue a silver eyelet to each hole. Let dry. String onto the silver ball chain.

## Tip

Take your time and don't try to squeeze large clumps of cotton through the hole; you risk breaking the edge of the hole. As you work in the water, the cotton ball will get softer with every movement and will come out more easily.

### Materials
### for assembling the necklace:

- Silver ball chain
- 14 large silver eyelets 1 cm ($^3/_8$ in.) in diameter
- Super glue

# Ice Queen Button

**Materials
for making the button:**

- White and silver polymer clay
- Silver ink pad
- Round cookie cutter 3 cm (1⅛ in.) in diameter
- Plastic food wrap
- Small glass or ceramic tile
- Toothbrush
- Flat-back crystal rhinestone
- Gem glue
- Needle
- Coarse salt

**1** Make a white sheet 2.7 mm thick and cover it with a sheet of plastic food wrap folded double. Use a cookie cutter to cut out a circle, then remove the plastic.

**2** Use a toothbrush reserved for working with clay to texture the edge of the circle.

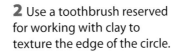

**3** Make a little ball of silver clay and flatten it between your hands.

**4** Place this silver disc in the center of the white circle. Press gently so the disc adheres without getting squashed.

**5** Use the glass square—which will be the baking surface—to press the shaped clay into the coarse salt. Make uniform marks.

**6** Gently rub the surface to remove the largest grains of salt. Ink the edges with the silver ink pad.

**7** Make two holes with the large needle before baking. Once the piece has cooled completely, use the gem glue to attach several rhinestones to the silver bead.

# Dots and Swirls Necklace

Learn cane techniques with a crowned spiral, and then try the mokume-gane technique, invented by Carole Valette, to create this colorful necklace and earrings.

**Materials for making the beads:**

- ⅛ brick of each color: red, orange, yellow, green, blue, violet, white, and gold
- Pearl Ex powder (or eyeshadow)
- Clipo child's building block or a Sculpey Technique Design Block
- Small glass tile
- Rigid craft knife
- Large needle

## CROWNED SPIRAL

**1** Condition each color of clay separately, starting with the lightest ones. Roll them into logs, then into strips of equal width.

**2** Use the knife to trim the edges straight and then stack the colors like stair steps, 5 mm apart.

**3** Roll up the whole thing into a spiral.

**4** Roll the spiral gently on the work surface to smooth out the surface, then cut the ends off neatly. Make the cane a little longer, then cut it in half: One piece will be used in the cane and the other will be used in the mokume-gane technique we'll look at immediately afterward.

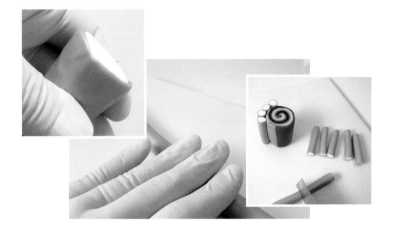

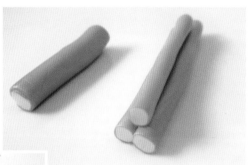

**5** To make the crown around the spiral: Condition the white clay and roll it into a thin rope, then wrap it in a sheet of gold clay (setting 3), crush the log a bit, then thin it out by rolling it on the work surface to obtain a rope about 5 mm in diameter.

**6** Save any leftover bits for use later on. Thin out the log again, cut it in three, and put the pieces together to form a triangle. The slices of this cane will be used to decorate the beads.

**7** Cut pieces of the rope to go around the spiral and press them into the clay so they adhere but don't get crushed. Make a thin rope of green and cut it into sections to place between the white-and-gold ropes.

**8** Roll out the cane on the work surface to reduce the diameter and smooth out the surface. Don't worry about the ends, which will almost certainly end up very misshapen. Once you trim off a bit, you'll find a very pretty motif inside the cane.

**9** Make three sizes of the cylinder to obtain motifs in varied sizes. Let them chill for at least three hours before slicing them.

# Mokume-gane

**1** Crush the other piece of the rainbow spiral (page 50) and apply a bit of metallic powder to the top so that the tool doesn't stick to it.

**2** Press firmly with the texture block, then cut off fine slices with a flexible craft knife.

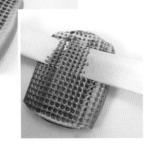

**3** Once the dotted effect is used up, apply the metallic powder again and repeat.

**4** Collect any leftover clay from the project and make it into a thick sheet, then fold the sheet in two to double the thickness.

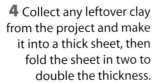

**5** To make balls of equal size, cut out pieces with a cookie cutter and roll them in your hands. Then add the dotted rainbow-pattern shavings.

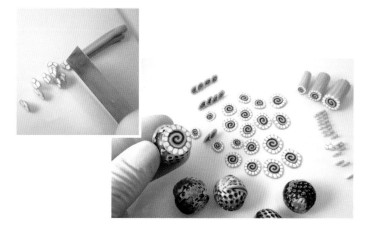

**6** Cut fine, regular slices from the different canes and place them on the balls.

**7** Roll between your hands to smooth out the surface.

**8** Slightly flatten each ball and make a hole from each side to the center. Then enlarge this hole using a bigger needle.

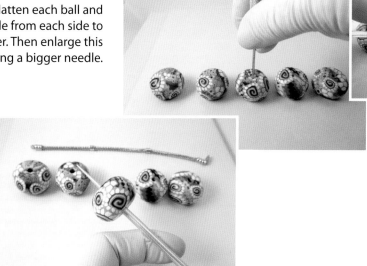

**9** Place an eyelet on either side of each bead, pressing them into the holes with the tip of your finger. Bake the beads.

**Materials
for assembly:**

- Snakeskin chain necklace with a clasp and extension chain
- Open jump ring 6 mm in diameter for attaching the charm
- 2 silver filigree balls 10 mm in diameter, with a large hole
- 4 small round silver beads (to place on either side of the large rings)
- 4 large closed jump rings, twisted silver, 11 mm in diameter
- Super glue

**1** After the beads have completely cooled, remove the eyelets and attach them with a dot of super glue.

**2** String the beads onto your chain. Between each pair of large polymer clay beads, add a small circular bead with a twisted jump ring.

**3** Add the clasp and extension chain decorated with a slice of cane matching that used for the earrings.

# Dots and Swirls Earrings

**1** For the dangling earrings, cut even slices 3 to 4 mm thick in the crowned spiral cane. Bake on a piece of cardboard.

**Materials
for assembly:**

- 2 long silver ear wires
- Two 4 mm seed beads in each color (red, orange, yellow, green, blue, and violet)
- 2 open jump rings 4 mm in diameter
- 2 open jump rings 6 mm in diameter

**2** Pierce the beads after baking, 3 mm from the edge, using a small drill bit turned between your thumb and index finger.

**3** Thread the seed beads onto the ear wires and attach these at each end with the two jump rings.

# Denim and Lace Necklace

Learn to imitate textiles such as lace and denim. The basic technique for a fabric look, made popular in polymer clay crafting by Sylvie Peraud, is presented to you here along with another way of imitating fabric.

**Materials for making the necklace:**

- 1 brick of pearly white Premo clay
- $^1/_2$ brick translucent clay
- Blue alcohol ink
- Scraps of lace and denim
- Fine felt-tipped acrylic pen (such as Posca)
- Round cookie cutters: 1.5 cm ($^5/_8$ in.), 1.8 cm ($^3/_4$ in.), 2.3 cm ($^7/_8$ in.), 3 cm ($1^1/_8$ in.), and 3.4 cm ($1^1/_4$ in.) in diameter
- Wet sandpaper: 400-, 600-, and 1000-grit
- Varnish, paintbrush
- 1 m (1 yd.) of silver chain: 2 lengths each of 9 cm ($3^1/_2$ in.), 23 cm (9 in.), 28 cm (11 in.), and 31 cm ($12^1/_4$ in.)
- 60 open jump rings 6 mm in diameter, to attach the drop beads
- 4 open jump rings 6 mm in diameter, clasp
- Polka-dot stamp
- Baby powder

## NECKLACE

All the drop beads are quite fine, thickness 3 on the clay machine. You need 19 drop beads on the short chain, 14 drop beads on the medium chain, and 24 drop beads on the long chain.

**1** Condition your pearly clay well by passing it through the clay machine several times until its color is uniform (see page 5). Texture both sides of the white pearly clay by folding the lace around the sheet.

**2** Remove the fabric and cut out the beads with the cookie cutter directly on the lace. Remove them from the lace carefully. Smooth the edges of the pieces with the tip of your finger, as needed, and place the beads on a piece of cardboard for baking, taking care not to misshape them.

**3** Color the remaining pearly clay with a few drops of blue ink and texture both sides by folding the denim around the thick sheet.

**4** Remove the top layer of fabric and color the clay by applying ink directly on the surface. Spread it across the clay with your finger and let it dry before repeating the process on the other side.

**5** Once the sheet is completely dry, cut out the beads with a cookie cutter and place them on the cardboard baking surface.

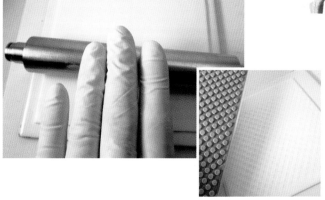

**6** To create a plumetis (fabric with raised polka dots) effect, place the translucent sheet on a ceramic square and very lightly mark the surface with the stamp dipped in baby powder.

## Tip

If needed, you can do this step during the day, holding the beads against a windowpane.

**7** Cut out the beads with different sizes of cookie cutters. Bake on the tile. After cooking, draw three little dots with the acrylic marker in each of the circles marked with the stamp. Let dry, then do the same thing on the other side, using the transparency of the clay to line up the dots. If you wish to create the dots with polymer clay, you can work as for the Buttercream Necklace on page 40.

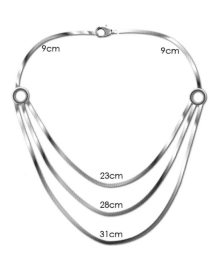

9cm          9cm

23cm

28cm

31cm

**8** Prepare your three-level chain. Drill holes in your beads 4 mm from the edge and attach them to the chain with jump rings.

# Denim and Lace Bracelet

The bracelet is made like the necklace, using the smallest beads attached to three 15 cm (6 in.) chains linked by a clasp. Decorate the extension chain with a small drop bead.

**Materials needed for the bracelet:**

- Chain: 3 lengths of 15 cm (6 in.)
- Extension chain
- Lobster claw clasp with an open jump ring
- 23 polymer clay drop beads
- 23 open jump rings 6 mm in diameter

# Steampunk Tag Pin

With simple stamps and a few colors of ink, you can easily make a variety of tags with a retro look.

**Materials
for making the tags:**

- Rigid craft knife, clay roller, clay machine
- 1 brick of white polymer clay
- Gold or yellow ocher clay
- Various chalk ink stamps
- Box of tag stamps
- Gauze compress
- Burnt sienna acrylic paint

## DISTRESSED TAGS

**1** For the tags, try to get Premo brand clay. This clay will remain flexible after baking and thus can be used very thin without the risk of breaking.

Condition your white clay and form it into a fine sheet (setting 3 on the machine). Place it on the unfolded gauze compress and go over it with the roller. The gauze compress placed underneath the sheet of clay will allow you to move the tags after working the clay, while texturing the backs of the tags.

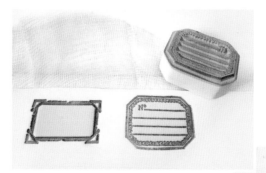

**2** Ink the stamps and mark the clay with different motifs.

**3** You can mix different colors on the same stamp.

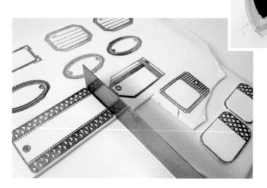

**4** Once the prints are made, remove the gauze and place the sheet of clay on a ceramic tile or a sheet of glass. Cut out the tags one by one with a rigid craft knife.

**5** Gather the leftover white clay and add a bit of gold or yellow ocher clay to it. Repeat steps 2 to 4 to obtain some beige tags.

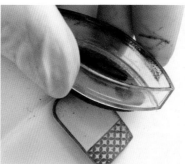

**6** Distress the tags one by one by coloring their edges with inks of different colors.

## Tip

To be able to move the tags without deforming them, pick them up by sliding a rigid craft knife blade underneath.

**7** Make holes in the tags with a large needle.

**8** Bake on pieces of cardboard, following the manufacturer's recommendations.

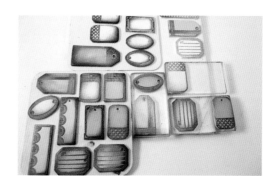

**9** After baking, apply a bit of acrylic paint on the backs of the tags to mark the weave of the gauze. Wipe the paint right away with a paper towel.

## ASSEMBLING THE PIN

**Materials
for assembling the pin:**

- Copper kilt pin, patinas for aging it
- 12 copper beads 4 mm in diameter
- 12 copper beads 2 mm in diameter
- 12 copper crimp beads
- Flat pliers
- 2 copper jump rings 6 mm in diameter
- Gear charm, key charm
- Scraps of cotton cord
- Super glue
- Scissors

**1** To give the brooch an antique look, use a product specifically created for aging or a blue patina. Proceed in the same way for the gear and the key.

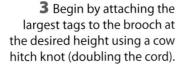

**2** Attach a length of cotton cord folded in half to each of your tags.

**3** Begin by attaching the largest tags to the brooch at the desired height using a cow hitch knot (doubling the cord).

**4** Continue along the length of the pin, using different colors of cord.

**5** At each cord end, thread on a 4 mm bead, a 2 mm bead, and a crimp bead to hold them in place. Cut off the excess cord.

**6** Turn the brooch over and place a dot of glue on each knot. Attach the key and the gear to the pin with the 6 mm jump rings.

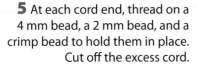

# Leading the Way in Crafts

**GREAT KNIT SWEATERS**
for Guys Big & Small

12 SWEA
Children's
to Men

*21 crocheted*
**TANKS + TUNICS**

Stylish Designs for Every Occasion

SANDI ROSNER

**KNIT tops** *for kids*

Irresistible Projects
for Girls & Boys
Ages 1 to 6

Muriel Agator

*fair isle*
**TUNISIAN CROCHET**

Step-by-Step
Instructions and
16 Colorful Cowls
Sweaters and More

Brenda Bourg

*cool* **CHUNKY KNITS**

26 Fast & Fashionable Cowls, Shawls, Shrugs & More for Bulky & Super Bulky Yarns

Tabetha Hedrick

*Bath* **KNITS**

30 Projects
Made to Pamper

Mary Beth Temple

**round loom KNITTING**
in 10 easy lessons

30 stylish projects
Nicole F. Cox

*soap making*
NATURALLY

Bev Missing

**POLYMER CLAY** *jewelry*

30 BRACELETS, PENDANTS,
NECKLACES, EARRINGS,
PINS, AND BUTTONS

Sophie Arzalier

*make your own*
**WREATHS**

FOR ANY OCCASION IN ANY SEASON

Nancy Alexander

YOKO SAITO'S
**Patchwork**
Bags & Accessories

25 Fresh Quilted Designs

**PEG LOOMS & WEAVING STICKS**

21 weaving projects, easy to complex
hat • dolls • toys • mats    button • band • cowls

Noreen Crone-Findlay

**NEEDLE FELTING**
FROM BASICS TO BEARS

with step-by-step photos and instructions
for creating cute little bears and bunnies from natural wools

Liza Adams

**NEEDLE FELTED**
*Tapestries*
MAKE YOUR OWN WOOLEN MASTERPIECES

16 PROJECTS
FROM SIMPLE TO ADVANCED
Neysa Russo

*make your own*
**SOAPS LOTIONS & MOISTURIZERS**

LUXURY
BEAUTY
PRODUCTS
YOU CAN CREATE
AT HOME

JINAIKA JAKUSZEIT

**CROCHETING rugs**

40 traditional, contemporary, innovative designs

Nola A. Heidbreder and Linda Pietz

## Discover inspiration and tips for your next project!